UNDERSTANDING ME

Who am I?

Janine McNally

ISBN - Paperback: 979-8-9896732-7-8
Second Edition: December 2025.
Printed in the United States of America.

Janine McNally, Th. M., D. Min.
Panama City, FL 32401
Janine@EquippingFireflies.com

WHO AM I?

Dear Parents

UNDERSTANDING ME " will lead your child through a basic theology of Man. It is the fifth in a seven-book series and addresses the big question, "Who am I?"

Our world says, "There's no right or wrong," "We decide what is true and right," and "We can create our own identity."

At a time when kids are going through enormous changes, they are confronted with ambiguity and confusion. They are asking many questions, including:

1. Who am I?
2. Am I loved?
3. Am I alone?
4. Why am I here?

This book handles each question from a Biblical perspective in an age-appropriate way and ends with the hope of a new life, a new body, and a new world for those who have trusted in Jesus.

You can participate in this discipleship process by encouraging your child and stepping in to help when needed.

Remember:

- Pray for your child that they will grow to know Jesus more each day.
- Don't expect your children to be perfect. Even though they may be saved, they are still sinners.
- Help them look up Bible verses and write answers in their books.

The extent to which your child will apply these lessons depends largely on the support and encouragement you provide as a parent.

We are praying for you.

> *"These commandments that I give you today are to be on your hearts. Impress them on your children.*
> *Talk about them when you sit at home, when you walk along the road, when you lie down, and when you get up."*
> Deuteronomy 6:6-7 [NIV].

UNDERSTANDING ME

WHO AM I?

Table of Contents

UNDERSTANDING ME

Who Am I?

Who are you?

I know.

You're "John Smith," or "Mary Adams," (or whatever your name is).

Or perhaps you answer,

- "I'm a student at First Elementary School," (or whatever your school is).

- "I'm a Bronco fan," (or whatever your favorite team is).

Perhaps you would list your hobbies or where you live.

- I'm a soccer player (or baseball or football).
- I love dance and ballet.
- I live in the city.

Or perhaps your answer was, 'I'm a Christian'?

Everyone needs a clear picture of who we are and an understanding of what that means.

UNDERSTANDING ME

We all need a unique identity. If we are not unique, we will just be another face in the crowd.

We won't stand out. We might as well be invisible.

Kids today are being taught that they can create and choose their identity.

- We can decide who we are.
- We can be who we want to be.
- Whatever we feel is true.
- We can control our future.

As we grow up, we want to know "who I am," "why I exist," and "what my purpose is."

- Who am I?
- Am I loved?
- What makes me special or unique?
- What value do I have?
- Do I have any influence?
- What was I made for?
- Do my choices really matter?

WHO AM I?

Your mom or dad might say, "You are you. And I couldn't imagine wishing you were anyone different."

Or perhaps Grandma gives you a really nice compliment.

But it doesn't really count coming from them.
They HAVE to love you!

What we really need to know is, am I loved by someone else?

- Someone who CHOOSES to love me.
- Someone who loves me NO MATTER WHAT.

Keep reading to find out if there is such a person!

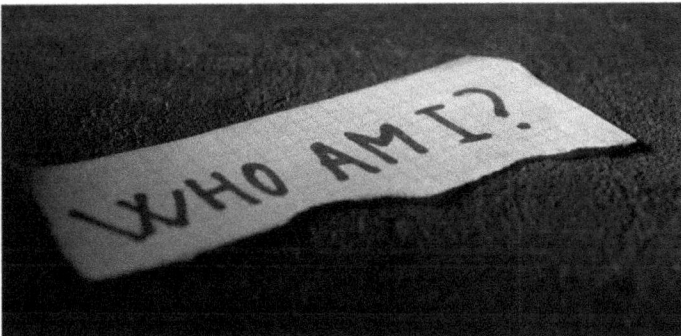

UNDERSTANDING ME

Our World

Our culture tells us to:

- Live for today. You only live once.

- Get what you want when you want it.

- You deserve to be happy all the time.

The problem with this thinking is that life is tough.

- Yes, you only live once, but that puts a lot of pressure on us to always get it right!

- You can't always get what you want.

- Pain and suffering are a part of being human, so the idea of being happy all of the time is unrealistic.

Following the world's advice might sound like freedom, but in reality, it just leaves us with uncertainty and failure.

We are left with anxiety and disappointment because the reality can't live up to the promise.

We are always afraid that we are missing out (FOMO).

Our World is Falling Apart.

- We are constantly bombarded with bad news.
- We hear about shootings, robberies, drugs,
- Families everywhere are broken.

My dad left my mom and, in the process, left us kids, too. It messed us all up, including him.

Perhaps your family is broken too – it's very common now to see moms trying to raise their family alone, or maybe dad is there physically but not really "there!"

Kids are struggling with anxiety and depression.

Everywhere we look, we are surrounded by confusion and uncertainty.

We hear so many different messages.

How do we know which ones are right?

Our responsibility is to be OK with whatever anyone chooses.

- Be tolerant.
- Be inclusive.
- Approve of all lifestyles and beliefs.

Yes, our world is damaged, dangerous, and scary.

How can we figure out who we are when everything around us is a MESS?

UNDERSTANDING ME

1. Our World Says: "There's NO Right or Wrong!"

The world says that there is no such thing as TRUTH.

You might have heard people say:

- Your "truth" is just different from my "truth."

- "What is right for you is right, and what is right for me is right."

- "Faith is OK if it works for you."

Whatever you believe might be different from others, but that's OK.

- We all basically believe the same thing.

- It will be OK if we try to be good people.

- Everyone is going to heaven.

What we believe about God is just a matter of personal opinion.

UNDERSTANDING ME

No one is wrong because there is no such thing as objective truth.

There is no black and white.
There is no right or wrong.
There are no objective standards.

2. Our World Says: "WE decide what is true and right!"

Since there are no "external" standards, we can decide what is right and wrong.

- No one can tell us what to do.

- We can choose whatever feels right.

- We can choose whatever we want and what makes us feel good.

- Everything depends on how we see things.

- Everything depends… on feelings, opinions, and desires.

The only things that matter are "love" and our preferences.

- How do we feel about something?
- What is our opinion?
- Will it offend anyone?

UNDERSTANDING ME

This message is seen on TV, in movies, in songs, in our schools, and online.

- "Be true to yourself."

- "Follow your heart."

- "If it feels good, do it."

- The "truth" is however I see it.

- All truth is relative: it is "MY truth," not "THE truth."

We are constantly influenced by celebrities, friends, social media, and political messages.

Do any of these sound familiar to you?

- "It's time to see what I can do to test the limits and breakthrough. No right, no wrong, no rules for me; I'm free." ("Frozen").

- "Your self-worth is determined by you. You don't have to depend on someone else telling you who you are." (Beyoncé).

- "Fairy Tales can come true. You just gotta make them happen. It all depends on you." (Tiana).

- "Whatever choice you make, let it come from your heart." (Queen Clarice: The Princess Diaries).

But what if our hearts are the problem?

Our hearts always chase the next big thing (stuff, experiences, friends, success). If we rely on our hearts, we will always be looking for more.

So…

- How do we recognize truth from lies?

- How can we figure out what is right and wrong?

- How do we know what is true?

Some people think that just believing something makes it true.

One person says that God exists, and another says He doesn't.

In today's world, they are BOTH right.

How is that possible?

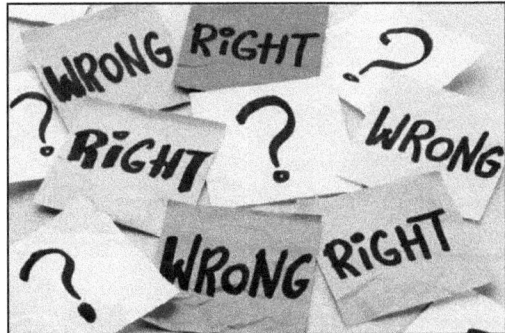

UNDERSTANDING ME

3. Our World Says: "We are basically GOOD!"

Since the world says that there is no right or wrong, then that means that we are not sinners.

There is no sin because there is no right or wrong.

So, there are no sinners!
Right?

We might not be perfect, but we're still "good."

That means that we do not need God.

- "Freedom and happiness are my goals."

- "Anything that stops me from reaching these goals (including traditions, religions, and rules) must be changed or destroyed."

- "And nothing, or nobody, can tell me otherwise."

How do you feel about this?

UNDERSTANDING ME

4. Our World Says: "We Can Create Our OWN Identity!"

The world tells us that we not only can create our own identity, but we MUST create our own identity.

- Who do I want to be?
- I can change who I am if I don't like how I am.
- I can change my label.

It's easy to do!

- I can just change my clothes.
- I can get a tattoo and be a part of the cool group.
- I can listen to different music or support different causes, and that will define who I am.
- I can change my job, my car, and even my gender.

Voila – I'm a new person!

And maybe, just maybe, I will be accepted if I just wear a different accessory or identify as a different person.

What do I prefer? What is the "in" thing today?

The problem is that the "in" thing changes constantly.

We are taught today that we not only can but MUST create our identity.

When we try to find or create our identity, it just leads to confusion, selfishness, and sinfulness.

5. Our World Says: "There is NO Male or Female."

Thinking that we can create our own identity has led to something we often see today.

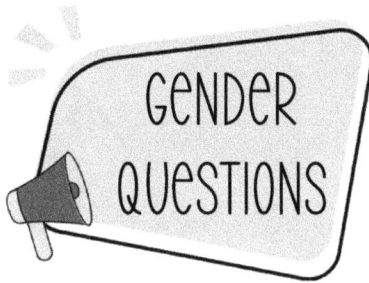

- Your friend decides she wants to be a boy from now on.

- You might see "Michael" in the cafeteria line, and the next day, it is "Mary."

- Jane and Julie walk hand-in-hand, and Steve wears a "dress."

The world tells us:

- "If I feel like a boy, I can be a boy."

- It's OK to be attracted to both guys and girls.

Perhaps some kids at school are putting pressure on you to be "gay."

UNDERSTANDING ME

The world tells you to be and do whatever you want because there is no right or wrong.

The voices are screaming at you to choose.

How are we supposed to figure this all out?

It's all so confusing.

There is an almost unlimited variation of pronouns now.

Depending on where you get your information, there are now 78 gender pronouns and 15 different "sexualities." It used to be so much easier when there were only two!

You can choose to be whatever you want.

When I was a young teenager, I hated being a girl. It seemed to me that boys had so much more fun.

- I loved climbing trees, playing sports, getting dirty, and playing marbles (you'll probably have to ask your grandparents what that is).

- I loved wearing jeans and sneakers and despised wearing dresses.

- I was a "tomboy" from head to my toes.

If I'd had a choice, I might have chosen to be a boy, but that choice was not mine to make.

It's Biology!

Regardless of what you hear from the world, your sex or gender was fixed when you were born.

My daughter found out three months into her pregnancy, by a blood test, that she was having twin boys. There was male DNA in her blood that confirmed both of their genders.

- Their genders weren't "assigned" at birth. They were already "boys."

- They were boys from the moment that they were conceived based on their chromosomes.

- Their external body parts were just visible evidence of their inborn gender.

But you might ask, what about people who are born with different body parts? For example, both male and female?

You are right.

There is a very small percentage of people who are born with medical conditions and abnormalities that are legitimately confusing.

Their physical anatomy is mixed up.
They have a physical developmental disorder.

But that is extremely rare.
Approximately one person out of every 10,000.

Gender Confusion

Did you know that gender confusion used to be a clinically diagnosed mental condition?

It was officially called "gender dysphoria" or "gender identity disorder." It was a genuine (and rare) mental condition.

Now, it is considered to be a "feeling of discomfort" or a "preference."

In today's world,

- We are not talking about physical or biological issues.

- We're not talking about diagnosed mental conditions or illnesses.

We're talking about preferences and choices!

- What do I want to be?

- What do I feel like?

UNDERSTANDING ME

In today's world,

- People choose to wear different clothes and grow or cut their hair to look more masculine or feminine.

- People choose to cross-dress and behave differently.

- People choose to change their names or their pronouns.

- Some people even choose to take hormones or even have surgery.

Being "Trans" is now trendy.

And you know what? It's a free country.

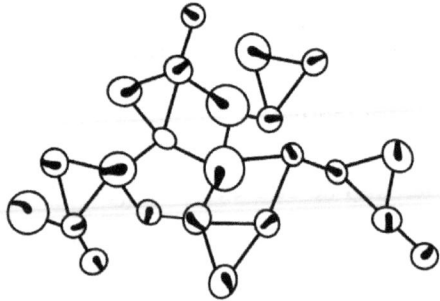

You can change how you express yourself, but nothing can change your DNA.

The really sad part about it all is that having a choice doesn't seem to be helping.

WHO AM I?

Changing your appearance doesn't help.
Behaving differently doesn't help.

The statistics tell us that:

- The average suicide rate across the United States is FOUR percent.

- The suicide rate in the transgender community is **FORTY** percent! TEN TIMES MORE!

Today's world is confusing and scary for everyone!

It's even more so if you are a kid learning to be an adult!

UNDERSTANDING ME

MY World

In the middle of all this mess, you are going through significant changes. Changing from a child to an adult is a big deal.

Growing up is a time of discovery, excitement, and confusion.

It's a time of unlimited possibilities and questions. It's a time of rapid physical, emotional, social, and spiritual changes.

UNDERSTANDING ME

Physical Changes

The most obvious change you will go through is physical. Your body and brain change more during these few years than at any other time.

Nothing is more humiliating than your voice cracking in the middle of a sentence or your friend telling you that you need to buy deodorant.

Most of us do not enjoy the process of puberty!

Is there anything about your body that you don't like? You can quickly list them all.

Our culture tells us that we need to make adjustments.

- We are careful about which photos can be posted on social media.

- We photoshop them if we can.

UNDERSTANDING ME

- We cover our blemishes with makeup.

- We work out at the gym.

- Some even go so far as to have surgery to fix a crooked nose or try to wipe out a few wrinkles.

Some say, "I hate my body."

It's not unusual to have a negative body image and feel really unhappy about your body.

I was always jealous of my little sister.

It was really silly little things, like her fingernails were a nice shape, while mine were square and stubby.

She was tall and slim. I was tall and not so slim. Her voice was "pretty." Mine sounded masculine.

She always seemed to know how to do her hair and makeup. I had no idea how to do either, so I always felt that I looked "average."

WHO AM I?

There were times I hated my body and the way that I looked.

And yet, the Bible tells us that our bodies, including all of their imperfections, are God's amazing, handmade gifts to us.

Read this Bible verse:

> *"For You [God] created my inmost being; you knit me together in my mother's womb."*
> Psalm 139:13 (NIV).

Who created you? G __ __.

Every part of our body was built by a perfect God who loves us more than anyone in the world. Nothing was an accident.

God carefully and purposefully gave you the body you were born with. It's a unique, hand-crafted work of art created by the Master Craftsman.

I have a framed picture on my bedroom wall. It is very special to me and has been hung in every house we have lived in.

And we have lived in a LOT of houses!

Why is it so special?
Because my sister made it for me.
It was handmade.

Years ago, she spent
hours and hours
cross-stitching a
beautiful piece of
art.

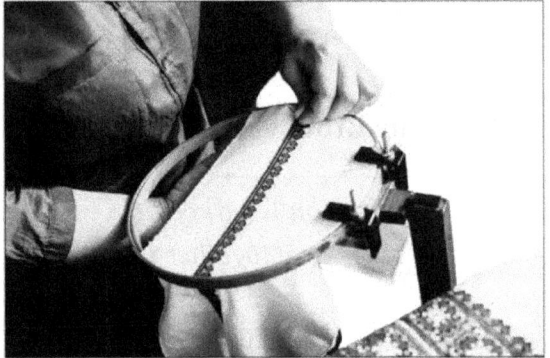

Those hours show her love for me. Every tiny stitch was placed in just the right position.

God didn't make a mistake when He "handmade" your body, nor did He give you the wrong one.

Read this Bible verse:

> "*I praise You **because I am fearfully and wonderfully made;** Your works are **wonderful**. I know that full well.*"
> Psalm 139:14 (NIV).

God's creation (you!) is W __ __ __ __ __ __ __ __ __.

It's easy to compare our bodies with other people's bodies.

We're too fat or too skinny, or too short or too tall.

However, rather than question God's judgment about His creation, we should thank Him for how He made us.

You know what?

The Bible tells us that Jesus, the **perfect** man, had an **ordinary** body.

> *"He [Jesus] **had no beauty or majesty to attract us** to Him, **nothing in His appearance** that we should desire Him."*
> Isaiah 53:2 (NIV).

Some people are so good-looking that others are drawn to them, but Jesus wasn't.

The movies made about Jesus all cast a good-looking actor, but they have it all wrong.

There was nothing amazing about Jesus's looks.

- Maybe His legs were scrawny.

- Maybe His ears stuck out, or His nose was too big.

- Maybe He had crooked teeth.

He was NOT good looking, but in God's eyes, He was PERFECT!

He was made just the way that God intended.

When sin entered the world, it ruined everything.
And because of that, "nobody" and no "body" is perfect.

The world might tell us what makes a good body, but God tells us what is true.

Remember:

- God handmade you!

- That makes you special.

- That makes you beautiful!

Jesus didn't try to be anyone else, and neither should we.

Mental Changes

Many changes take place in our brains as we grow.

Did you know:

If you were to look at a brain scan of a two-year-old or a three-year-old and compare it to a scan of an eleven-year-old, they would look almost the same.

- At **ages two and three**, a child's brain is getting ready to learn using language.

- At **ages eleven to twelve**, a preteen's brain is beginning puberty and entering the teen years.

During the preteen years, your brain is getting ready for adulthood and becomes malleable [changeable] again.

Very similar monumental developmental shifts are happening.

- Preteens become more verbal. They like to talk.

- Preteens' understanding will progress from concrete to abstract thinking.

- Preteens become more logical in thought.

- The preteen years begin a time when memories are more formative. Most of what you experience will now be remembered forever.

These are HUGE changes!

Social Changes

So, OK – God loves me and thinks I'm great. But what about people?

- "Am I good enough?"
- "Do I fit in?"
- "Will anybody ever be attracted to me?"
- "What are my strengths?"
- "How do I make up for my weaknesses?"

As we grow up, we experiment, explore, and try on different hats.

- We make new friends and grow apart from others.
- We sometimes win, and sometimes we fail.
- We love our family, but we also want to be independent.

It's a HUGE time of change.

We begin to branch out from our family and express our individuality and independence.

We still love our family, but we want independence.

UNDERSTANDING ME

- Our peer group has become very important to us.
- Peer approval has become more important to us.

Cliques emerge.
There are the "popular" kids and the "athletic" kids, and they all hang out in their groups.

Other kids are left out.

Fashion and friends begin to define what's "cool."

Your friends become more important than anyone.
They are the ones you listen to now.

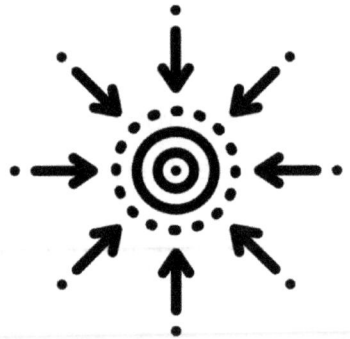

Our social focal point is shifting.

And at the same time, we tend to be very self-conscious, self-absorbed, and egocentric.

We think that our feelings are unique.

- "No one has ever felt like this before."

We think that everyone is focused on us.

- "Everyone is watching me."

WHO AM I?

At any age, but at this age especially, time with family and friends is critical.

- We all want to feel valued and loved.

- We all want to belong and feel connected.

We shouldn't have to change who we are to fit in with the group.

We should be accepted for who we are.

That is what "belonging" is.
Being loved and accepted just the way we are.

Texting and messaging might feel like true friendship, but it's actually artificial.

When you text (on WhatsApp, Facebook, Snapchat, Instagram, or whatever app you use), you are showing something that is entirely untrue and does not reflect who you are.

You can hide behind your screen.

UNDERSTANDING ME

It's easy to pretend. You show only the parts of yourself that will give you the best response. It's easy to say anything you want.

- You can talk about things you wouldn't usually talk about.
- You can be rude and fight ugly.
- You can bully people without being confronted.
- You can break up with a friend.
- You could even propose.

It can hinder real interaction because we are so busy on our phones.

We forget how to have an honest, face-to-face conversation. Or perhaps we've never learned.

When you talk in person, it's different.

You have to explain your words and your feelings. The other person can see your reactions, emotions, and feelings.

When we spend all of our time on screens, it means less real-person interaction.

- We need to learn practical social and interpersonal skills.

- We need to know how to develop healthy friendships.

It's not that technology is bad.

We need it.

But we must also find a balance between the computer and real people.

UNDERSTANDING ME

Emotional Changes

During these years of change, your emotions will go up and down, sometimes for no reason.

- One day, you might feel sad.

- The next day, you're on top of the world and don't even know why.

There will be times when you feel insecure or rebellious.

You might feel invincible. Nothing and nobody can stop you!

Everyone else (especially your parents) is wrong. It's always someone else's fault (not yours).

Emotional issues can be really serious during this time of life.

- Most kids feel lonely at times.
- Some kids struggle with anxiety.

- Some struggle with depression and eating disorders.

- You might know someone who has tried cutting themselves to make the pain go away.

- You might even know someone who has thought about suicide or even tried.

You might have even felt some of these feelings.

If you are struggling with some of these more serious issues, you need to find someone you can talk to.

Not a friend your own age, but a trusted adult.

Spiritual Changes

This is also the time when kids begin to question their beliefs.

Perhaps you've asked some of these questions.

- Is God really there?
- Is church useful or not?
- Is the Bible really true, or is it just a bunch of fairytales?
- Do I have time for this, or are the other interests in my life more valuable?

Questions like these are typical.

You are beginning the transition from following your parents and what they believe to discovering what you believe for yourself.

Is it all really true?

Perhaps you've grown up in the church and always believed in God.

But now, you notice people at church preaching and teaching about loving God, and then you see them acting like everyone else in the world.

You notice your parents are not as "perfect" as you once thought.

They seem like such hypocrites.

You wonder if all this church stuff is worth it.
Is it real?

Our world is a mess.
Your world might feel like a mess, too.

But thankfully, "God's world" is not!

God's World

Rather than finding the answers to our questions in the world and other people's opinions, let's see if we can find out what the Bible says.

God's world is very different from our world.

The voices we hear coming from social media and the internet are different from what the Bible, our church, and, often, our parents are telling us.

Most things we hear are the opposite of what the Bible teaches us.

When we're young, deciding which voice is right and which we should ignore isn't easy.

You will never go wrong if you follow what the Bible says.

UNDERSTANDING ME

1. The Bible says, "Truth is TRUTH - for EVERYONE."

The Bible says that there IS right and wrong!

Read this verse:

> *"All Your words are **true**. All Your laws are **right**."*
> Psalm 119:160 (NIRV).

God's word is T __ __ __ and R __ __ __ __.

Relativism is a big word that you might not have heard of.

It means the idea that truth, knowledge, morality, and other judgments are not **absolute** (either right or wrong) but are **relative** to (or depend on) an individual's perspective, culture, or historical context.

- For example, you might believe that God exists, but your friend doesn't.

- You might believe that there is a heaven, but your neighbor doesn't.

- You might believe that you're a sinner, but your teacher doesn't.

TRUTH-LIE

Relativism means that there is no truth. It all depends on what you think and feel.

While the world tells us that everything is relative, that is not true.

There IS a right and a wrong.
There IS truth.

Let's look at an example.

We all agree that murder is **wrong**.
To believe this, we must believe in some level of truth, some definition of right and wrong, good and evil.

Murder is **wrong**.
Sin is **wrong**.

And if something can be wrong, then there must be things that are right.

God is truth.
God's truth applies not just to some people.
It applies to **everyone**.

2. The Bible says, "GOD decides Truth, not Us!"

The Bible is our unchanging standard for success in life.

> *"Use the truth to make them holy. **Your word is truth.**"*
> John 17:17 (NIRV).

God has laid out His rules for living according to His plan and purpose.

He made it clear what is right and what is wrong in the Bible.

If we want to live well, we need to follow His guidelines.

When we choose the wrong direction, there will be consequences.

God is the ultimate authority.
He created everything and controls everything.

He decides what is true, not us!

UNDERSTANDING ME

3. The Bible says: "We ARE sinners!"

The unfortunate reality is that we are all sinners.
We are imperfect, and if left to our own devices, we will mess up everything!

- Have you ever told a lie?
- Have you ever disobeyed your parents?
- Have you ever said something mean to someone?
- Have you ever stolen something?

We all have.
We are all sinners.

The Bible says:

> *"For all have sinned and fall short of the glory of God."*
> Romans 3:23 (NIV).

This verse tells us that A __ __ have sinned.
Every one of us.

Just look at the world and how messed up it is.
That is what happens when sinners try to decide what is truth.

UNDERSTANDING ME

4. The Bible says: "God has ALREADY created our identity!"

God has already created our identity.
We don't need to invent or make it up.

Who we are (our identity) is already established in Jesus.

- There is no need to create it.

- There is no need to "get it right."

- There is no need to "discover" it.

It has already been established by God.

It is not based on our accomplishments, failures, preferences, or character.

Who we are is found in God and who He is, not in our feelings or performance.

Let's be honest!

We all like to be good at something.
It makes us feel good about ourselves.

- If you're smart, you want to be a straight-A student.

- If you're skinny, you try out for cheerleading.

- If you're athletic, you try out for the football team.

- If you're good-looking, you want to be the quarterback's girlfriend.

We try to look good to others so that they will think that we are "special."

1. We are superior to others.

2. We are popular.

3. We are "cool."

There's nothing wrong with wanting to excel in sports or academics, but finding our worth in an activity or a person is never good.

It is dangerous to measure our value by what people think or say.

We want people to say nice things about us.
We want to be valued by someone.

The good news is that **you are**!

You have value and dignity, not because of what you do, but because of **Who you belong to**.

- You belong to God.

- He created you.

- Therefore, YOU HAVE VALUE!

The BIG Questions

Have you ever asked one of these questions:

1. Who am I?

2. Am I loved?

3. Am I alone?

4. Why am I here?

They are some of the most important questions that we will ever ask.

Let's see if we can find answers for them in the Bible.

UNDERSTANDING ME

Question 1: Who Am I?

We already talked a bit about our identity.
Let's see what the Bible has to say about who you are.

Let's begin at the beginning.

The Bible tells us that God created the world in six days.
After making all the animals, He was still not happy.

He wanted to create something unique and special.
So, He created people.

Read these Bible verses:

> "Then God said, "Let us make **mankind** in our image, in our
> likeness, so that they may rule over the fish in the sea and the
> birds in the sky, over the livestock and all the wild animals,
> and over all the creatures that move along the ground."
> So, God created **mankind** in His own image, in the image of
> God He created them; **male and female He created them**."
> Genesis 1:26-27 (NIV).

Fill in the blanks.

God created M __ __ __ __ __ __.

God created mankind in His own I __ __ __ __.

UNDERSTANDING ME

You might wonder, "Who am I?"

You are special.

God created you exactly how He wanted you to be.

Yes. Freckles and all.
Skinny or chubby.
Tall or short.

God made you perfectly.

Exactly how He wanted.

1. God Created Mankind "in His Image."

You have been uniquely designed and created in God's image.

What does it mean to be "created in His image?"

God doesn't have a physical body with two arms, two legs, and a head.

So, what does it mean to be created in His image?

It means that you have intellect, emotions, and a will.

- You can think and make choices and decisions like God.

- You can feel sad, hurt, angry, or happy, just like God.

- You can show love and compassion.

- You want justice when someone is hurt.

- You have a free will to love God.

- You have an eternal soul that lives forever.

You are not the same as plants or animals.

You are like a mirror that shows people what God is like.

UNDERSTANDING ME

You are a work of art that shows how amazing God is.

You are a reflection of God.

2. God Created Them "Male and Female."

Read this verse again.

> *"So, God created mankind in His own image, in the image of God He created them; **male and female** He created them."*
> Genesis 1:27 (NIV).

Did you notice?

God created them; M __ __ __ and F __ __ __ __ __.

God created TWO genders!

The Bible is very clear.
There are two genders, not 78 or 15.
Just TWO!

Male and female.

That is not a very popular opinion today.

But it's the truth.
God's truth!

UNDERSTANDING ME

Did Sin Ruin Everything?

Sin messed up things – that's for sure. But it didn't destroy God's image.

It just messed it up a bit.

The mirror might be cracked, and the image a little distorted, but it is still there.

The Bible tells us that EVERYONE was made in God's image – not just people who have believed in Him.

Read this verse.

> "With the tongue, we praise our Lord and Father, and with it, we curse human beings, who have been made in God's likeness."
> James 3:9 (NIV).

Fill in the blanks.

Some people P __ __ __ __ __ God.

Some C __ __ __ __ people.

But everyone is made in God's image, even those who don't love God.

UNDERSTANDING ME

The image is no longer perfect.

- Our thinking is warped.

- Our talking is twisted.

- Our relationships are broken.

- Our motives are selfish.

The mirror is cracked, but God created you for a purpose.

He created you with a plan in mind.

Keep reading to find out what that is!

Question 2: Am I loved?

Yes! You are loved!

The Bible tells us that you are loved with an everlasting love.

Read these verses and draw a circle around the words that tell us how God feels about us.

> *"I have loved you with a love that lasts forever. I have kept on loving you with a kindness that never fails."*
> Jeremiah 31:3 (NIRV).

> *"God chose us to belong to Christ before the world was created. He chose us to be holy and without blame in His eyes. He loved us."*
> Ephesians 1:4 (NIRV).

God loves us more than anything!

Keep reading to find out how much.

UNDERSTANDING ME

1. You Are the VERY Best Part of God's Creation!

What did God say about His creation?

Read these verses below and draw a circle around the word that is repeated in each verse.

> *"God saw that the light was good, and He separated the light from the darkness."*
> Genesis 1:4 (NIV).

> *"God called the dry ground "land," and the gathered waters He called "seas." And God saw that it was good."*
> Genesis 1:10 (NIV).

> *"The land produced vegetation: plants bearing seed according to their kinds and trees bearing fruit with seed in it according to their kinds. And God saw that it was good."*
> Genesis 1:10 (NIV).

> *"God made two great lights—the greater light to govern the day and the lesser light to govern the night. He also made the stars. God set them in the vault of the sky to give light on the earth, to govern the day and the night, and to separate light from darkness. And God saw that it was good."*
> Genesis 1:17-19 (NIV).

> "So, God created the great creatures of the sea and every living thing with which the water teems, and that moves about in it, according to their kinds, and every winged bird according to its kind. And God saw that it was good."
> Genesis 1:21 (NIV).

> "God made the wild animals according to their kinds, the livestock according to their kind, and all the creatures that move along the ground according to their kind. And God saw that it was good."
> Genesis 1:25 (NIV).

Fill in the blanks below.

God saw that the light was G __ __ __.

God saw that the dry land and waters were G __ __ __.

God saw that the vegetation was G __ __ __.

God saw that the sun, moon, and stars were G __ __ __.

God saw that the sea creatures and birds were G __ __ __.

God saw that the animals and livestock were G __ __ __.

Everything God created was just as He wanted it.

WHO AM I?

Read this verse.

> "So, God created mankind in his own image, in the image
> of God he created them; male and female he created them."
> Genesis 1:27 (NIV).

God finished His creating on day six.

What did God create on Day six?   M __ __ __ __ __ __.

What did God say when talking about His creation on the
sixth day?

> "God saw all that He had made, and it was very good. And
> there was evening, and there was morning—the sixth day."
> Genesis 1:31 (NIV).

He said the words "V __ __ __   G __ __ __."

His creation of people on the last day was more than
good.

It was VERY good.

We are the best of God's creation

You are the pinnacle of God's creation.

UNDERSTANDING ME

2. You were ADOPTED into God's Family

Do you know anyone who was adopted?
Why do you think they were adopted?

Adoption is always a **choice** made by parents who desperately want to love a child.

God adopted us into His family.
We are His children.
You are His child!

Read this verse.

> "So, **He [God] decided long ago to adopt us. He adopted us** as His children with all the rights children have. He did it because of what Jesus Christ has done. It pleased God to do it."
> Ephesians 1:5 (NIRV).

What did God give us?

All of the R __ __ __ __ __ that children have.

Why did He adopt us?

Because of what J __ __ __ __ has done.

How did He feel about it?

It P __ __ __ __ __ __ Him.

UNDERSTANDING ME

When you wonder if God loves you, remember:

- You are not valuable to God because of how you look or what you see in the mirror.

- You are not valuable because of what you do.

- You are not valuable because of how many "A's" you get on your report cards or how many trophies are on your dressers.

- You are not valuable because you are a part of the "popular" kids at school.

You are valuable because of WHO you belong to!

You are a child of the KING of KINGS!

You are ROYALTY!

Question 3: Am I Alone?

You are NEVER alone!

Read this verse and draw a circle around all of the places you could run away from God.

> *"Where can I go from Your [God's] Spirit? Where can I flee from Your presence? If I go up to the heavens, You are there; if I make my bed in the depths, You are there. If I rise on the wings of the dawn, if I settle on the far side of the sea, even there, Your hand will guide me; Your right hand will hold me fast."*
> Psalm 139:7-10 (NIV).

What does the writer say about God?

His hand will G __ __ __ __ you.

His right hand will hold you F __ __ __.

Where is God? E __ __ __ __ W __ __ __ __.

God promises that He will never leave you.

Draw a circle around the things in this verse that cannot separate us from God.

> *"For I am convinced that neither death nor life, neither angels nor demons, neither the present nor the future, nor any powers, neither height nor depth nor anything else in all creation, will be able to separate us from the love of God that is in Christ Jesus our Lord."*
> Romans 8:38-39 (NIV).

Can anything separate us from God? (Circle One)

YES?	NO?	NOT SURE

Read this verse:

> *"The Lord Himself goes before you and will be with you; He will never leave you nor forsake you. Do not be afraid; do not be discouraged."*
> Deuteronomy 31:8 (NIV).

God promises to NEVER L _ _ _ _ you or

F _ _ _ _ _ _ you.

Rest assured.
You are NOT alone!

Question 4
Why Am I Here?

Here are a few of the reasons.

Read these verses and see if you can find out why we were made.

1. We were made to K __ __ __ God.

The most important reason is that we know God.

> *"Now this is eternal life: that **they know You**, the only true God, and Jesus Christ, Whom You have sent."*
> John 17:3 (NIV).

2. We were made to L __ __ __ God.

> *"Jesus replied: "'**Love the Lord Your God with all Your heart and with all Your soul and with all Your mind.**' This is the first and greatest commandment."*
> Matthew 22:37-38 (NIV).

3. We were made to F __ __ __ __ __ God.

> *"And what does the Lord require of you? To act justly and to love mercy and to **walk humbly with your God**."*
> Micah 6:8 (NIV).

4. We were made to do G __ __ __ W __ __ __ __ __.

> *"For we are God's handiwork, **created in Christ**
> **Jesus to do good works,** which God prepared in*
> *advance for us to do."*
> Ephesians 2:10 (NIV)

5. We were made to T __ __ __ __ God.

> *"**Trust in the Lord** with all your heart and lean not*
> *on your own understanding; in all your ways submit*
> *to Him, and He will make your paths straight."*
> Proverbs 3:5-6 (NIV).

6. We were made to L __ __ __ O __ __ __ __ __.

The first commandment we were given was to love God.
Here is the second one.

> *"And the second is like it: '**Love your neighbor**
> **as yourself.'** All the Law and the Prophets hang*
> *on these two commandments."*
> Matthew 22:39-40 (NIV).

WHO AM I?

Humans are pack animals.

- We need each other.
- We need friends.
- We need relationships.

When I was young, I heard kids ask, "Will you be my best friend?"

How many "best friends" do you have? _____

The friendships lasted a few weeks, and then there were new "best" friends.

- The athletic kids chose the "jocks."
- The popular kids chose the "cool" kids.
- The "nerds" chose the "brainiacs."

The best one I heard was, "Will you be my boyfriend (or girlfriend")?

At age 10 or 11, that meant nothing except that it you hung out together. Maybe you held hands.

But it made you feel "wanted."
You felt valued.

UNDERSTANDING ME

Being a part of a group is also super important.
If you aren't in a group, you are an outsider.

Are you in a "group?"

Friendships are sometimes more about what we can GET
than what we can GIVE.

We **want** to feel wanted.
We **want** to feel like we belong.
We **want** to be "popular."

But God created us to LOVE others.
God created us to love **everyone**!

- Those who are popular **AND** unpopular.

- Those who are attractive **AND** unattractive.

- Those who are "normal" **AND** not normal.

Jesus loved others.

- He didn't just stick with people like Him.

- He loved people when no one else did.

We are ALL valuable in God's sight and all worthy of
love.

WHO AM I?

Remember what God said about His creation of mankind in Genesis chapter one? He said it was VERY good.

God created Adam and put him in the most perfect garden.
But something was missing.

Draw a circle around what God said about Adam being alone.

> *"The Lord God said,*
> *"It is not good for the man to be alone."*
> Genesis 2:18 (NIRV).

What was God's answer to Adam's loneliness?

> *"I will make a helper who is just right for him."*
> Genesis 2:18 (NIRV).

He would make a H __ __ __ __ __ for him.

Living in a perfect garden wasn't enough.
Adam needed someone to share it with.

God made us to need people.
We need friends.

God made us to love others.

Do you wish that you had more friends?

Read this verse.

> *"A man who has friends must himself be friendly."*
> Proverbs 18:24 (NKJV).

The Bible says that F __ __ __ __ __ __ __ people will have friends!

If you truly love others, not just for what you can get for yourself, then you will have friends.

The trouble is that we often want friends so that WE feel good, not so that we can help THEM.

We're made to be like God - to love others, even if they are very different from us.

We're not made only to have one best friend and to leave others out.

Life is better when we are a good friend to others.

WHO AM I?

Figuring Out Who I Am

1. Take Your Time

Figuring out who you are and what your specific purpose is will take a lifetime.

You may think that you have it all figured out, but it takes learning, growing, and time.

As you get older, you will try new things, and you will discover gifts and abilities that you didn't know you had.

You will make mistakes and learn and grow from your experiences.

Eventually, you will get a good idea of who you are and why God created you.

There are a few things we can do that can help speed the process along.

WHO AM I?

2. Watch Others

Watch the kids who are around your age.

- What decisions are they making?
- Are they good decisions?
- What consequences are they facing when they make bad choices?

Watch the adults in your life and the way they live.

- Who do you admire and respect?
- What is it about them that you like?

Watch someone who is living "well."

- Follow their example.
- Spend time with them.
- Ask them questions and listen to their answers.
- Take their advice.

Most kids ignore good advice.

They are determined to make their own choices, even when strongly advised otherwise.

Save yourself some hurt. Listen to those who love you.

WHO AM I?

3. Know Your Creator

I remember learning a verse for a Bible club I attended as a kid.

> *"Remember Your Creator in the days of Your youth."*
> Ecclesiastes 12:1 (NIV).

When should we get to know our Creator, God?

In the days of our Y __ __ __ __.

If we can get to know God while we are young, it will save us much trouble later.

When we begin our relationship with Christ, we can start to see ourselves the way God sees us. We will KNOW who we are!

How do we get to know God?

As we said earlier, the Bible tells us that we are all sinners.

> *"For **all have sinned** and fall short of the glory of God."*
> Romans 3:23 (NIV).

"Sin" means "to miss the mark."

Whenever we lie, hate, lust, gossip, or do anything wrong, we have missed the standard God has set.

The Bible also tells us that the penalty for sin is death.

> "For the wages of sin is **death**."
> Romans 6:23 (NIV).

The penalty for our sin is D __ __ __ __.

Death is another way of saying that we are separated from God.

God is Holy (Perfect), so our sin separates us from Him.

The good news is that Jesus died to pay our sin penalty. The Bible says:

> "God demonstrates His own love for us in this:
> While we were still sinners, **Christ died for us**."
> Romans 5:8 (NIV).

What did Christ do for us?

He D __ __ __ for us.

UNDERSTANDING ME

Someone had to die and pay the penalty of "death."

The Bible says that Jesus took our place.

He paid the penalty we deserved (because of our sin),
placed it on Himself, and died in our place.
He paid our sin penalty.

Three days later, Jesus came back to life to prove that sin
and death had been beaten and that His claims to be God
were true.

The good news is that God has provided a way for us to
be with Him forever.

The Bible says:

> "For God so loved the world
> that He gave His One and Only Son, that whoever
> **believes in Him** shall not perish but have eternal life."
> John 3:16 (NIV).

Fill in the blanks.

The Bible tells us that whoever B __ __ __ __ __ __ __ in

Jesus will be not P __ __ __ __ __.

We will have E __ __ __ __ __ __ L __ __ __.

What does it mean to "believe?"

"Trust" is another word for "belief."
We must **trust** Jesus Christ to get us to heaven.

- Some people think that they can work their way to heaven.

- Some people think they are already "good" enough.

But trying to work your way to heaven is not possible.
We will **never** be "good" enough.

God doesn't want our good works.
- Going to church won't help pay the cost.
- Being baptized won't save us.
- Being good won't help pay the cost.

The penalty is DEATH, and the only way to pay the penalty is by dying.

Jesus did that for us.

We must **believe** (trust) that when Jesus died on the cross for our sins, He paid our FULL sin penalty.

100% of the cost.

Remember:

- We can't pay the penalty with G __ __ __ works.
- We cannot W __ __ __ our way to heaven.

You must trust in Jesus Christ ALONE, and God will **give** you eternal life as a FREE gift!

It's a gift.
You don't work for a gift.
If you try to pay for it, it is no longer a gift.

Your Future World

Living in our world today is hard.
It's no wonder that so many are struggling.

You face constant suffering and pain.
There is bad news around the clock.

The good news is that one day, we will have a new life, a new body, and a new world.

This life is temporary.
When compared with "forever," it is just a blip.

Read this verse.

> "What is your life? You are a mist that appears for a little while and then vanishes."
> James 4:14 (NIV).

Our life is a M __ __ __.

Have you noticed that when it is foggy, the fog lifts when the sun comes out?
It only lasts for a little while.

Our life is just like that. It will be over before you know it.

And this is what we have to look forward to.

1. A New Life

Once you have trusted in Jesus to save you, you are given a new life.

> *"You have started living **a new life**."*
> Colossians 3:10 (NIRV).

> *"Therefore, if anyone is in Christ, the new creation has come. The old has gone, the new is here!"*
> 2 Corinthians 5:17 (NIV).

You are a N __ __ C __ __ __ __ __ __ __ __.

When we become a Christian, we get a brand new start.

> *"For you have been born again."*
> 1 Peter 1:23 (NIV).

You are B __ __ __ A __ __ __ __ __.

You are born into **God's** family.

- God gives us a new nature and a whole new outlook on life.
- He is with us, walking with us as we begin this new life.

Jesus changes everything in us.

WHO AM I?

2. A New Body

You not only get a new life, but you will also be changed and given a new body.

> "So, **we are being changed** to become more like Him [Jesus]."
> 2 Corinthians 3:18 (NIRV).

> "By His power, He will **change our earthly bodies**. They will become like His [Jesus'] glorious body."
> Philippians 3:21 (NIRV).

Our new bodies will be just like J __ __ __ __.

When Jesus came to earth, His body was like ours.

- He could cut his finger or scrape His knees.

- He could twist His ankle or lose a tooth.

- He could die on a cross.

But when He came back to life, His earthly body was changed to a heavenly one.

And one day, we will get a new "heavenly" body too, just like Jesus.

3. A New World

One day in the future, we will have a new world.
One day, all of the pain and suffering in the world will end.

All the bad will be replaced with good, and sin will be gone.

- We were made for more than just our own pleasure
- We were made for a better world than this one.
- We were made for heaven.

All of the difficulties and disappointments we have faced in this life will be more than made up for by an eternity of living with Jesus in heaven.

Read this verse.

> *"But we know that when Christ appears, **we will be like Him.** That's because we will see Him as He really is."*
> 1 John 3:2 (NIRV).

When will this happen?

When Christ A __ __ __ __ __ __.

One day, Jesus will come back to earth and take us to heaven.

One day, we will be like Jesus.

Sin and death will be gone.
Our struggles will be over.
Our doubts will vanish.

We will be with God.

Read these verses.

> *"And God Himself will be with them and be their God.*
> *'He will wipe away every tear from their eyes.*
> *There will be no more death.' And there will be no*
> *more sadness. There will be no more crying or pain.*
> *Things are no longer the way they used to be."*
> Revelation 21:3-4 (NIRV).

Fill in the blanks.

There will be no more T __ __ __ __.

There will be no more D __ __ __ __.

There will be no more S __ __ __ __ __ __.

There will be no more C __ __ __ __ __ or P __ __ __.

WHO AM I?

We will see Jesus' face!

- There will be no secrets to hide.

- There will be no sin to feel ashamed of.

- There will be no confusion or fear.

There will be only joy.

It almost seems too good to be true, but this is the future that God promises to those who have trusted in Him.

When you're trying to understand who you are, always remember:

- I am a child of the KING.

- I am loved.

- I am NEVER alone.

- I have a purpose.

So, if you ever wonder, "Who am I?" you now know the answer.

UNDERSTANDING ME

Congratulations

You have completed "UNDERSTANDING ME." Write your name and date on your certificate, and have your parent or a teacher sign it.

Certificate of Completion
Awarded to

_____

On _____   _____   _____
         Month   Day   Year

For completing UNDERSTANDING ME.

Presented by _____
                    Signature

UNDERSTANDING ME

Note To Parents

Most parents want to do the right thing, but so often, they are either too busy or overwhelmed. You need to be a good role model to set an example for your children. They are watching.

Here are some suggestions to get you started.

- Make sure your children have a Bible of their own. Make sure it's age-appropriate. They can't read it if they don't understand it (see the following page recommendations).

- Provide notebooks for each child to write down what they learn. Encourage them to write down their prayer requests and the answers to their prayers.

- Encourage them to read their Bible for five minutes every day. We suggest that you begin with the book of John.

- Encourage them to write down any questions and ask you or their Sunday School teacher.

- Make time each day to read your own Bible. Kids learn by watching you. Set a good example for them to follow.

UNDERSTANDING ME

Choosing The Best Bible for Your Child

Here are some recommendations for Bibles to help your kids get excited about God's Word!

MAKE AN AGE-APPROPRIATE CHOICE.

If you want your children to enjoy reading the Bible, buy one that is easy to read, attractive, and engaging. Too often, kids struggle to look up verses at church in a Bible that has tiny print, is in a hard-to-read translation, and has no pictures or illustrations to draw them in.

Paul wrote to young Timothy,

"And how **from childhood** you have been acquainted with the sacred writings, which are able to make you wise for salvation through faith in Christ Jesus." 2 Timothy 3:15 (NIV).

Timothy began studying the Bible as a young child. As parents, we want our kids to know and love God's Word, so buy them a Bible that they will understand.

BUY A BIBLE FOR EACH CHILD

Each child needs their own copy of the Bible. As parents, we spare no expense to buy our kids whatever they need to succeed in school or sports. Do the same for God's Word. Buy them a Bible that they will love to read.

The New International Version for Young Readers (NIrV), the New International Version (NIV), or the English Standard Version (ESV) are good translations for kids.

It's one of the most important investments you can make in your child's Christian education and spiritual development.

RECOMMENDED BIBLES FOR CHILDREN

Here are some examples of recommended Bibles available today.

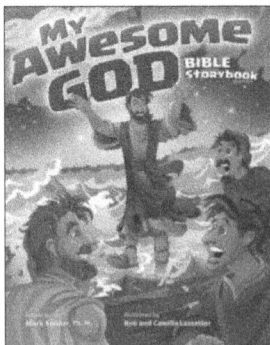

PRESCHOOL
My Awesome God Storybook
The MY AWESOME GOD Storybook Bible is ideal for parents who want to read the key stories of the Bible to their young children. This Bible includes a topical index and helpful discussion questions.

YOUNGER ELEMENTARY

NIrV Adventure Bible for Early Readers – For Ages 5–10

This is a simpler version of the children's NIV Bible created for younger readers.

One of the easiest translations is the New International Reader's Version (NIrV). The NIrV is the young reader's edition of this fun, interactive Bible that helps children learn about what they are reading through helpful information presented throughout.

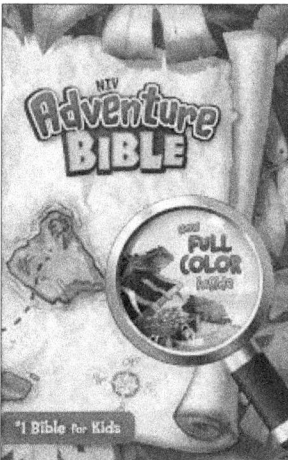

NIV Adventure Bible – For Ages 8–11

The bestselling NIV Adventure Bible® will get kids excited about reading the Scriptures! Your kids will be captivated by the full-color features that make it fun and engaging to read the Bible and memorize their favorite verses.

CSB Explorer Bible

This Bible reads similarly to the NCV translation and is filled with fun activities, maps, and images that your kids will not want to put down.

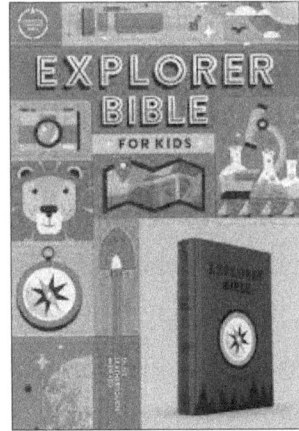

UPPER ELEMENTARY

Your preteen children can really start to master the Word of God! Here are some exciting options!

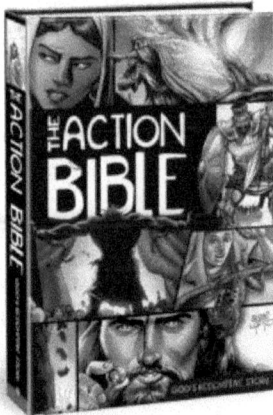

The Action Bible

The Action Bible presents the entire Bible in cool comic book illustrations. Kids will read it cover to cover many times over.

The Action Bible Study Bible

The creators of the Action Comic Bible also published a Study Bible edition in both the NIV and ESV.

The Action Study Bible is the complete text of the Bible, with select illustrations from the Action Bible throughout.

UNDERSTANDING ME

The Understanding Life Series.

UNDERSTANDING SALVATION is a short workbook designed for children ages 7-12 to use independently or with a parent.

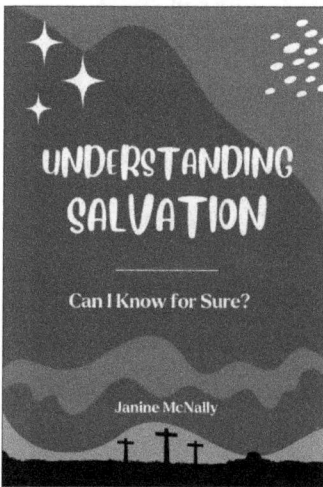

It presents the good news of Jesus in a clear and easy-to-understand way that will help them know FOR SURE that they will live with Jesus in heaven one day.

Children will learn the key principles of salvation, teaching the "Bad News" (sin) and "Good News" (Jesus), along with Bible verses and simple illustrations.

This 120-page book will help them deepen their understanding of God's grace and begin their relationship with Him.

UNDERSTANDING BAPTISM is a 95-page workbook designed for children ages 8-12 to use independently or with a parent or leader.

It is intended for those who have already expressed their belief in Jesus for salvation and have asked about being baptized.

This book answers these questions.

- How can we be saved?
- Can I be sure I am saved?
- What is baptism?
- Why should I be baptized?
- When should I be baptized?
- What happens during a baptism?

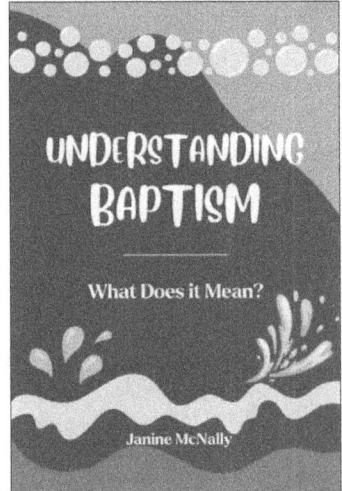

UNDERSTANDING GOD is the third book in the "Understanding Life" series for Kids, written for children ages 9-12.

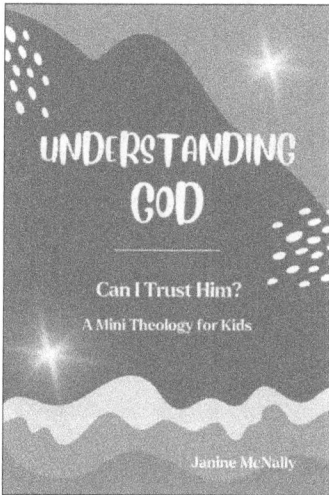

Children are asking questions every day about God, the Bible, salvation, life, death, the afterlife, angels, demons, and more.

We need to be prepared with answers, or they will look elsewhere.

This 135-page book answers the following questions.

1. What is God like?
2. How did He create the world?
3. Who Created God?
4. Who is the Holy Spirit?
5. How can Jesus be God but also be God's Son?
6. Why does God let bad things happen?
7. Can God make mistakes?
8. Does God Love Me?

This book can be used as a training resource for your volunteers or as a parent.

UNDERSTANDING the BIBLE is the fourth book in the series.

When your child asks the tough questions, do you have answers for them? Do they know how to read the Bible and apply it in their lives?

- How do we know the Bible is true?
- Is the Bible trustworthy?
- How do we know that it is really God's Word?

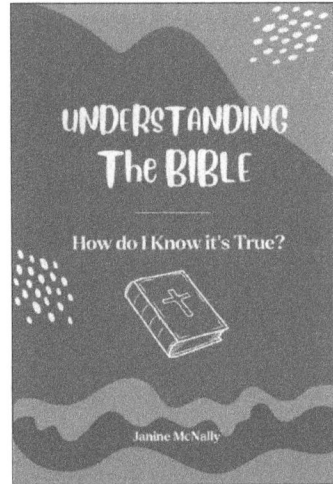

Written for children ages 8-12, this 120-page book teaches some basic Bible apologetics.

The content includes:
Three Big Words:
1. Inspiration - Written by God and Man
2. Inerrancy - No mistakes
3. Preservation

The Bible's Structure
How to Have a Quiet Time
How to Memorize God's Word

UNDERSTANDING ME addresses the big question, "Who am I?" in this 120-page book for kids ages 9-12.

Our world says, "There's no right or wrong," "We decide what is true and right," and "We can create our own identity."

At a time when kids are going through enormous changes, they are confronted with ambiguity and confusion.

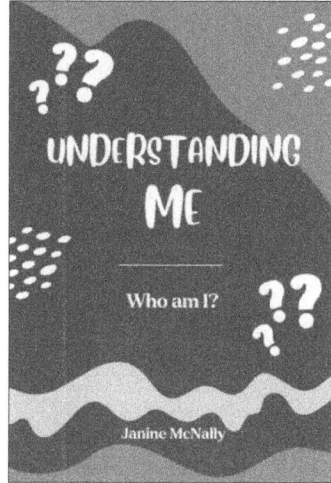

1. Who am I?
2. Am I loved?
3. Am I alone?
4. Why am I here?

Each question is handled from a Biblical perspective and ends with the hope of a new life, a new body, and a new world for those who have trusted in Jesus.

UNDERSTANDING HARD QUESTIONS is the sixth book in the "Understanding Life" series for kids.

It answers 56 of the most common questions asked by kids from a Biblical perspective and in an age-appropriate way.

- Who created God?
- Does God speak to people?
- Will God stop loving me if I keep sinning?
- How did Jesus perform miracles?
- Why do people get sick and die?
- Why did my parents get divorced?
- Can Christians lose their salvation?
- How can God forgive murderers?
- Why is sex outside of marriage wrong?
- Are there more than two genders?
- Can I be sure that I will go to heaven?

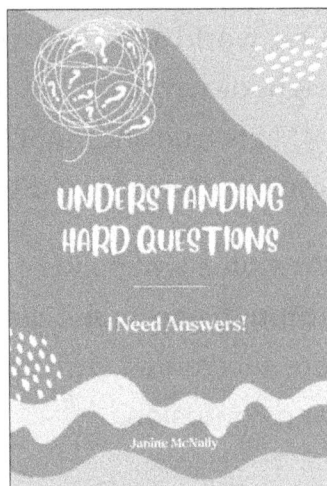

Written for kids ages 9-12, this 165-page book answers these questions using basic Bible apologetics.

UNDERSTANDING LIFE & DEATH is written for children ages 8-12 and addresses the questions that arise when a child experiences the death of a loved one.

- Why Do People Get Sick and Die?
- What Happens After You Die?
- If God Loves Me, Why Did My Dad Die?
- What is Heaven Like?
- Will Everyone Go to Heaven No Matter What They Believe?
- Do People Who Never Hear About Jesus Go to Heaven?
- Is Hell Real?
- How Could a Loving God Send People to Hell?
- Why Did God Create Satan?

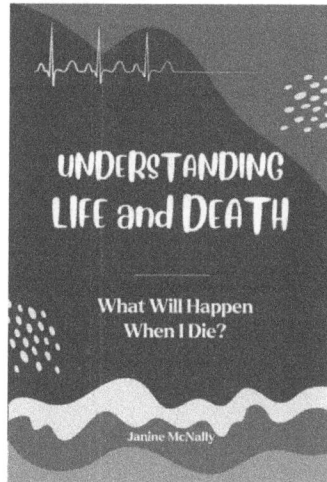

UNDERSTANDING LIFE and DEATH

What Will Happen When I Die?

Janine McNally

This 120-page book answers these questions and more from a Biblical perspective in an age-appropriate way. It aims to provide help and hope in times of sadness and grief.

UNDERSTANDING ME

About the Author

Originally a high school teacher in her native Australia, Janine McNally has partnered with her husband for many years of pastoral ministry.

Janine graduated with a Master of Theology from Dallas Theological Seminary and a Doctor of Ministry from Grace School of Theology.

She is the author of "When You See Fireflies—Equipping Leaders and Parents to Minister Effectively to Generation Alpha," the "Understanding Life for Kids" series, seven devotional books for kids ("10 Minutes with God"), and "STEPS to Knowing Jesus" for kids and preteens.

She passionately believes in reaching kids for Jesus and enlightening leaders and parents about Generation Alpha and beyond.

Janine and Gary have been married for thirty-two years and live in Panama City, Florida.

They have three grown children, Hannah (married to Kevin), Jonathan (married to Brayton), and Jami Grace.

They also have three beautiful grandchildren, Grayson, Hunter, and Emerson.

WHO AM I?

About the Ministry

Janine McNally directs the operations of **Equipping Fireflies**, a non-profit dedicated to providing gospel-centered resources that proclaim a message that will grab the attention of this generation, break the magnetic attraction of the increasingly dark world, and lead children to the Light.

THE STORY BEHIND THE NAME

"When do we have to come inside?"
"When you see the fireflies."

Our kids loved to play outside, but as night began to fall, it was time to come in, where it was safe. Each evening, for a short time, the fireflies would light up our entire backyard. Their unmistakable glow was the signal that it was time.

Our world has become much darker. We desperately need the kids and their families to hear the call. "Come inside where it's safe." The world is rapidly becoming bleaker as the generations race by, yet our children are running towards the night.

We must proclaim a message that grabs their attention,

one that they understand and that will break the magnetic attraction of the increasingly dark world.

"You are the light of the world.
Let your light shine before others that they may see your good deeds and glorify your Father in heaven."
Matthew 5:14; 16

OUR PASSION

Statistics show that most Christians trusted Christ between the ages of 3 and 12. Our passion is to reach children for Jesus and serve, equip, and encourage Children's Ministry leaders and parents.

THE GOOD NEWS

When Jesus died on the cross, He did EVERYTHING that God requires for us to go to heaven when we die."

EQUIPPING FIREFLIES

Lighting the Way for the Next Generations.
www.equippingfireflies.com

WHO AM I?

"And these words which I command you today shall be in your heart. You shall teach them diligently to your children, and shall talk of them when you sit in your house, when you walk by the way, when you lie down, and when you rise up.
You shall bind them as a sign on your hand, and they shall be as frontlets between your eyes. You shall write them on the doorposts of your house and on your gates."
Deuteronomy 6:6-9

www.ingramcontent.com/pod-product-compliance
Lightning Source LLC
Chambersburg PA
CBHW061737020426
42331CB00006B/1269